— P E O P L E T O K N O W —

AMY TAN

Author of
The Joy Luck Club

Barbara Kramer

ENSLOW PUBLISHERS, INC.

44 Fadem Road	P.O. Box 38
Box 699	Aldershot
Springfield, N.J. 07081	Hants GU12 6BP
U.S.A.	U.K.

Library of Congress Cataloging-in-Publication Data

Kramer, Barbara.
    Amy Tan, author of The Joy Luck Club / Barbara Kramer.
       p. cm. — (People to know)
    Includes bibliographical references and index.
    Summary: Explores the life and career of author Amy Tan, from her childhood in Oakland, California, through her struggle to accept her Chinese heritage, to her career as a writer.
    ISBN 0-89490-699-2
    1. Tan, Amy—Juvenile literature. 2. Women novelists, American—20th century—Biography—Juvenile literature. 3. Chinese Americans—Biography—Juvenile literature. [1. Tan, Amy. 2. Authors, American. 3. Women—Biography. 4. Chinese Americans—Biography.] I. Title. II. Series.
PS3570.A48Z76   1996
813'.54—dc20
[B]   95-41601
                                          CIP
                                          AC

Printed in the United States of America

10 9 8 7 6 5 4 3 2

Illustration Credits:
Adam Scull/Globe Photos, Inc., p. 75; Andrea Renault/Globe Photos, Inc., p. 4; Harry Benson, p. 7; Jim McHugh/Visages, pp. 29, 45, 54; Michael Ferguson/Globe Photos, Inc., pp. 20, 65, 83, 89; ©Robert Foothorap, pp. 37, 57, 85, 92; Ron Davis/Shooting Star, p. 87; San Jose City College, p. 26; Sonoma County Library, p. 17; Susan Farley ©1991 New York Newsday, p. 78.

Cover Illustration: ©Robert Foothorap

Contents

Amy Tan

1

A Celebration

When Amy Tan's first book, *The Joy Luck Club*, hit *The New York Times* bestseller list, she celebrated. It was not the usual kind of celebration: "everyone thought I was out at a fancy place having champagne," she said.[1] Instead, she was shooting pool. "It's what I like to do when I'm not writing," she explained.[2]

Tan says playing pool is a lot like writing. In both activities you have to stay focused. "If you're thinking about what somebody expects, or what someone's thinking as they're watching you, or what you're going to look like, you're in trouble," she says.[3]

Tan knows what she is talking about. In the billiards room of her home in the Presidio Heights area of San Francisco, California, there is a trophy with a shark on top. It is proof of her skill. "Shark" is the name given to those who play the game well.

Tan had reason to celebrate the success of *The Joy Luck Club*. It made *The New York Times* bestseller list in April 1989 and stayed there through November of that year. The paperback rights for the book were sold for a reported $1.2 million.

Those were impressive figures for a first book, but perhaps even more impressive was the fact that the book was written at all. Even as a child Tan had hoped to write fiction one day, but she never believed she could be successful at it. "I never dreamed of being a published author," she told a reporter for *Newsday*. "I was Chinese; I was a girl. It was as preposterous as a Chinese girl dreaming of becoming president of the United States."[4] The practical side of her personality told her that she could not make a living writing fiction. It was something she would have to do as a hobby.

As an adult, she put her dream aside and turned to the more lucrative field of business writing. It was only when she realized she was working too many hours a week and needed to find a way to relax that she decided to start writing fiction.

The Joy Luck Club explores the relationships between four Chinese women and their American-born daughters. It is divided into sixteen short stories. Each of the stories is about an episode in the life of one of the mothers or daughters. The stories are about love and conflict

Amy Tan playing pool. It is what she likes to do when she is not writing.

between mothers who want their daughters to embrace their Chinese heritage and daughters who want to be "100% American."[5] It is a subject Tan has learned about firsthand.

The daughter of Chinese immigrants, Amy Tan had spent her youth trying to deny her heritage. She was more interested in fitting in with her American friends. She once spent a week sleeping with a clothespin on her nose trying to change her Asian appearance because she thought it set her apart from other children.[6] All she got from that episode was a sore nose. She was embarrassed by her mother's broken English and by her Chinese customs. By the time she was a teenager, Amy had rejected "everything Chinese."[7]

Tan did not fully appreciate her Chinese heritage until she was thirty-five years old. That year, she visited China for the first time. The trip was just as her mother told her it would be. "When my feet touched China, I became Chinese," she said.[8]

Tan began writing *The Joy Luck Club* as a way to understand the mother-daughter tensions she and her mother had experienced. "When I was writing, it was so much for my mother and myself," she said. "I wanted her to know what I thought about China and what I thought about growing up in this country."[9]

Although the book is about Chinese women, critics have pointed out that it is not just a Chinese story. In an article for *Newsweek*, Dorothy Wang reported that "her insights into the complexities of being a hyphenated American, connected by blood and bonds to another culture and country, have found a much wider audience than Tan had ever imagined."[10] Julie Lew of *The New York Times* wrote, "the women in *The Joy Luck Club* could belong to any immigrant group."[11] Reviewer Rhoda Koenig noted, "I was amused by how Jewish the Chinese mothers sound."[12]

Tan has heard from teenagers all across the country who say they are facing the same pressures she wrote about in her book. They tell her they do not understand their mothers, they are not interested in learning about their heritage, and they do not want to feel different.

In a letter to Tan, a Missouri teenager wrote, "A few ignorant students mocking me would always cause me to wish that I had blonde hair instead of dark brown. You wrote many beautiful things in your book that made me realize that I was lucky to have two cultures."[13]

The Joy Luck Club was translated into seventeen languages, including Chinese, and was later made into a movie. For Amy Tan, the dream of being a fiction writer—a dream she once thought was out of her reach—had finally come true.

2

"Blessing From America"

Amy Tan's Chinese name is An-mei. It means "blessing from America."[1] It was a fitting choice for the only daughter of parents who had immigrated to the United States from China only a few years earlier.

Amy was born in Oakland, California, on February 19, 1952. Her parents, John and Daisy Tan, had come to the United States from China in the late 1940s to escape the Communist takeover of their country. They left behind a homeland that had been torn apart by decades of war.

The Nationalist party had been in power in China since 1913. However, the future of that government was constantly threatened by two different forces—Japan and the Chinese Communists.

During World War I (1914–1918), Japan had seized

control of German holdings in northeastern China. After the war, Japan was allowed to keep those territories. It was part of the peace settlement called the Treaty of Versailles, which was formulated by the Paris Peace Conference in 1919. With the rise to power of new military leaders in the early 1930s, the Japanese in China began to advance into new territories. They gained control of Manchuria, along the eastern edge of China, and began moving inland to Inner Mongolia.

The other threat to the Nationalist government was the emergence of the Communist party. The first Communists began to appear in China in 1919. On May 4 of that year, students gathered in Beijing to protest the terms of the Treaty of Versailles. Their demonstrations opened the door for Communist leaders, who found support for their ideas among the students. By 1931, the Communists had set up their own government in southern China.

Chiang Kai-shek was the leader of the Nationalist party. He had come into power in 1926 after the death of the previous leader, Sun Yat-sen. Because Chiang could not fight both Japan and the Communists at the same time, he decided to concentrate on the threat of Communism.

In 1934, he drove the Communists out of southern China and forced them north to Manchuria. This year-long six-thousand-mile trek became known as the Long March. More than one hundred thousand

Communists began the march, but only about twenty thousand survived. During that time, Mao Tse-tung became the leader of the Chinese Communist party.

For the next ten years, China was plagued by civil war and a Japanese invasion. At one point in the late 1930s, the Nationalists and the Communists actually joined forces to fight Japan. In spite of their efforts, when World War II began in 1939, Japanese troops occupied many large Chinese cities, including Beijing and Shanghai.

During World War II, China sided with the Allied forces against Japan. When the Japanese attacked Pearl Harbor on December 7, 1941, the United States also joined the Allied forces. Japan surrendered to the Western Allies in August 1945, after the United States dropped atomic bombs on the Japanese cities of Hiroshima and Nagasaki. At that time, there were about 1.2 million Japanese troops in China. When Japan surrendered to the Western Allies, the Japanese troops in China were ordered to stop fighting. The United States sent these soldiers back to Japan.

Soon after the war, full-scale fighting broke out between the Chinese Communists and the Nationalists. The Chinese Civil War continued for almost four years. On October 1, 1949, the Communists established the People's Republic of China and made Beijing their capital. In December of that year, Chiang Kai-shek fled to the island of Taiwan, where he reestablished the Republic of China.

Amy Tan's parents met in China in the mid-1940s. They fell in love, but there was a complication—she was already married. Chinese women had few rights at that time. Marriages were arranged for them by their families. Daisy Tan, whose maiden name was Tu Ching, was forced into a marriage to a man who was an abusive husband. She eventually left him, which was a crime in China, and for that she spent three months in prison.

John Tan had been educated in Beijing as an electrical engineer. Since he had been schooled by Christian missionaries, he could speak English, and during World War II he worked for the United States Information Service. That wartime experience made it easier for him to immigrate to the United States in 1947.

John Tan planned to get settled in the United States and work things out so that Daisy Tan could join him after she got out of jail. However, it was hard for him to begin life in a new country. He was haunted by the difficulties Daisy Tan was facing in China. "He felt responsible for her suffering," Amy Tan later explained. "He felt that if he placed his hopes in God, she would be saved and allowed to join him."[2]

His prayers were answered. Daisy Tan succeeded in getting a divorce after twelve years of marriage. Then she escaped on the last boat out of Shanghai in 1949 before the Communists took control of China.

With the Communist takeover, the once friendly relationship between the United States and China came to an end. The United States refused to recognize the People's Republic of China. Instead, they supported Chiang Kai-shek's Nationalist government on Taiwan. The new immigrants were completely cut off from their relatives and friends who remained in China. They did not know if they would ever see each other again.

John and Daisy Tan were married shortly after her arrival in the United States. John Tan had been offered a scholarship to study engineering in the United States, but he turned it down and enrolled at Berkeley Baptist Divinity School to become a minister. It was his way of thanking God for his wife's safety.

The Tans had three children—their daughter, Amy, and two sons, Peter and John, Jr. Peter was born in 1950; Amy in 1952; and John, Jr., in 1954. Daisy Tan worked nights as a vocational nurse while raising her family. Vocational nurses, or licensed practical nurses as they are called in some states, work under the direction of physicians or registered nurses.

In America, Amy's parents tried to keep their Chinese traditions. When Amy was young, her mother spoke to her "half in English, half in Mandarin."[3] Mandarin is the language spoken in most of China. After Amy started school, her mother still spoke to her in Chinese, but Amy would answer in English. It was an early act of rebellion for a daughter who wanted to be like her American friends.

John and Daisy Tan knew that America offered their children many opportunities. They set high goals for their daughter. When Amy was five, they bought a piano so that she could begin piano lessons. When she was six, she was part of an education study done in Oakland, California. The psychologist who conducted the study concluded that Amy "was smart enough to become a physician."[4] To her parents, that meant that she would grow up to be a doctor. Since they thought the brain was the most important part of the body, they decided she would be a neurosurgeon. "From the age of 6, I was led to believe that I would grow up to be a neurosurgeon by trade and a concert pianist by hobby," Tan once told an interviewer.[5]

The family moved often—each time John Tan found a better position as a minister. They lived in Oakland, Fresno, and Berkeley, California, and in various suburbs of San Francisco, before finally settling in Santa Clara, California. Although they never left the Bay Area, each move meant a change in schools. "I moved every year, so I was constantly adjusting," Tan said.[6]

Many immigrants from China settled in segregated communities like Chinatown in San Francisco. However, the Tans lived in integrated neighborhoods. From third grade on, Amy was the only Chinese-American girl in her class. She was always aware that she was not like the other students. "I remember trying to belong and feeling isolated. I felt ashamed of being different and ashamed of feeling that way," Tan said.[7] She worried about what kind of treats her mother would bring to school for her birthdays. She was afraid it might be something Chinese that would embarrass her in front of the other students.[8]

Amy entered her first writing contest when she was eight years old. She liked to read, and most of her reading material came from the local library. Unfortunately, the library was old. When Amy was in third grade, the building was found to be unsafe for library patrons. It had to be shut down.

A campaign was started to raise funds for a new building. Part of the campaign was to have children write essays about what the library meant to them. Amy entered the contest.

She patterned her essay after one of her father's sermons. She felt his sermons were honest, and he always used simple language.[9] She began her essay, "My name is Amy Tan."[10]

Another thing she remembered about her father's sermons was that he always asked for money at the end. She did that too. She clinched her plea by saying that she was donating seventeen cents to the library fund. It "was all the money I had in the world," Tan later said.[11]

Although Amy was only eight years old, she already seemed to sense the importance of writing with emotion.

This is the library where Amy Tan's father used to take her until it had to be closed down. When she was eight, Amy wrote an essay as part of a campaign to raise money for a new library.

She told how much she loved to read and how she enjoyed trips to the library with her father. Then she expressed her disappointment that the library had to be closed. "I missed it like a good friend," she wrote.[12]

Students from the elementary schools and junior and senior high schools in the area entered the contest. There were 148 entries altogether representing three different age groups. Six winners, a girl and a boy from each group, were selected. Amy won in the elementary school division. Her essay was published in the Santa Rosa *Press-Democrat*, along with the essays of two other winners.

In spite of that early literary success, Tan says that she was steered away from pursuing English and writing by both her teachers and her parents. They encouraged her in subjects like science and mathematics—subjects in which she did well on standardized tests. According to Tan, Asian-American students traditionally do better on the science and mathematics portions of those tests. She believes that it is because the tests are culturally biased. In an essay Tan later wrote, called "Mother Tongue," she explained, "Math is precise; there is only one correct answer. Whereas, for me at least, the answers on English tests were always a judgment call, a matter of opinion and personal experience."[13]

Although Amy was a good student, she sometimes struggled to make sense out of her studies. She tried to identify with the pilgrims and pioneers in her history books, but they had nothing to do with her own past. American history "was just a barrage of facts that had no relevance to me," she said.[14]

The United States has been called a melting pot, which means that various races and cultures have been blended to produce a so-called American culture. Amy was learning that this was not entirely true. In the process of trying to be accepted, she found, she was "deliberately choosing the American things—hot dogs and apple pie—and ignoring the Chinese offerings."[15]

Amy's attempts to be like her American friends caused tension between her mother and herself. Generations of teenagers have complained that their parents do not understand them. They point out the difference in their ages and the way times have changed since their parents were young. For Amy and Daisy Tan, those problems were multiplied. They not only had generational differences, there were cultural differences as well.

Tan says what she believes hurt her mother most was that Amy did not feel more responsibility toward her family. "She couldn't understand why I would want to be with my friends more than with her or with my family."[16]

When Amy was fourteen, she became infatuated with a boy named Robert who was not Chinese. Much to Amy's dismay, her mother invited Robert's family to their house for dinner on Christmas Eve. Tan later wrote about that episode in an essay for *Seventeen* magazine.

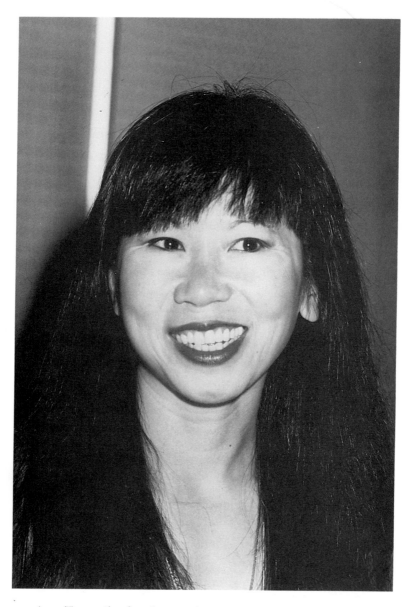

Amy Tan smiles for photographers. As a child she thought her Oriental characteristics made her different from the other children in her class at school.

She said that instead of turkey, her mother served raw fish. "The kitchen was littered with appalling mounds of raw food," Tan wrote.[17] During dinner, Amy's family used chopsticks and reached across the table to help themselves to the platters of food, while Robert's family waited for the food to be passed to them. Amy's ultimate embarrassment came when her father ended the meal with a loud belch. "It's a polite Chinese custom to show you are satisfied,"[18] he explained, but Amy could only think about how her family must have looked to Robert.

After their guests left, Amy's mother gave her an early Christmas present. It was a beige miniskirt, which was in fashion at the time. Then Daisy Tan said, "You want to be the same as American girls on the outside. But inside you must always be Chinese. You must be proud you are different. Your only shame is to have shame."[19]

It would be many years before Amy Tan fully understood her mother's words, yet that evening she did learn one thing: Her mother did know how embarrassed Amy was, and she understood Amy's feelings. Looking back on that time, Tan realized how her mother had decided what to serve for that dinner—"she had chosen all my favorite foods," Tan wrote.[20]

In spite of generational and cultural differences, the Tans lived comfortably in California, until a double tragedy shattered their lives.

3

A Rebellious Daughter

When Amy was fifteen, her older brother, Peter, and her father both developed brain tumors. Amy spent much of that year in hospitals, a witness to their suffering.

As the daughter of a Baptist minister, Amy had learned all about praying and about the Baptist ideas about God's will. On the other hand, she had also learned about Chinese luck and the superstitions that were part of her Chinese heritage. Amy saw her mother draw on all those resources trying to find a reason for what was happening to her family.

"My mother looked for answers everywhere," Tan recalled.[1] She wondered if their house was out of alignment, or whether her family had to pay for something bad they had done in the past.

Daisy Tan never gave up hope that her husband and

son might recover. She searched for ways to make it happen. Would chemotherapy cure them? Or did they need to change the direction the wind blew through their house? At one point she brought in a Pentecostal faith healer, believing that might be the answer.

Nothing helped. Amy's brother and father both died within about six months of each other. It was a terrible irony that their deaths were caused by brain cancer, since John and Daisy Tan had hoped that their only daughter would one day become a brain surgeon.

After the deaths of her son and husband, Daisy Tan listened to the advice of family and friends who told her to leave their "diseased" home in Santa Clara. Daisy Tan also thought about Amy's father, who had died without ever having a real vacation. She decided that she and her remaining two children needed to see more of the world before anything else happened to them. She began to make plans to travel.

Before they left, when she and Amy were having a disagreement, Daisy Tan made a shocking confession. She told Amy that she had three daughters from her first marriage. They were living in China.

Daisy Tan had hoped that someday she would be able to bring her Chinese daughters to America. That dream became an impossibility in 1949, when the United States ended its official relationship with China.

"Three obedient daughters, beautiful girls who could

speak Chinese," Tan later said. "I was crushed. I didn't see them as anything but competition."[2]

Daisy Tan and her children, Amy and John, set sail for Holland, taking with them a list of English-speaking schools. They settled in Montreux, Switzerland, where Amy and her brother attended school at the Institut Monte Rosa Internationale.

Amy had been uncomfortable being the only Chinese student in her classes in the United States, and she was a minority in Switzerland, too. There were very few Asians in Europe at that time, but Amy did not feel so much like an outsider there. Most of the students were from other countries. They were children of ambassadors and wealthy businesspeople from a variety of countries. "They were *all* different," Tan remembered.[3]

Daisy Tan expected that after all her family had been through, her daughter would become more obedient, but that did not happen. The unhappiness of losing her father and brother and the shock of learning that she had three half-sisters in China only made Amy more rebellious.

She got in with a bad crowd in Switzerland and began dating a young German man. There were rumors that the young man had connections with known drug dealers. Daisy Tan decided to find out the truth about him. She hired a private detective.

The detective discovered that the rumors were true: The young man was involved with drug trafficking. He was also an escapee from a German mental hospital. Tan says that her mother then "engineered the biggest drug bust in the history of Montreux."[4] She even had her daughter brought before the local magistrate.

Later, when Amy saw the young man again, she realized she was not interested in him anymore. He had just been a part of her rebellion.

The Tans spent a year in Switzerland. At school Amy took extra courses and managed to graduate from high school early. Then Daisy Tan, Amy, and John returned to San Francisco.

In the fall of 1969, Tan left for Linfield College in Oregon. It was a small Baptist school, one of two colleges that her mother had selected for her. Tan enrolled as a premed student.

At Linfield, Tan had a blind date with an Italian-American man named Louis (Lou) DeMattei. They were well suited to one another, and at the end of the school year, they both moved to San Jose, California. Tan enrolled at San Jose City College and changed her major from premed to a double major in English and linguistics, the study of language—its structure, history, and use.

Tan's decision to change her major was one her mother could not accept. For years, Daisy Tan had dreamed that one day her daughter would become a doctor. In an interview with David Streitfield of the *Washington Post*, Tan talked about her mother's reaction

A view of the San Jose City College campus at the time when Amy Tan enrolled in 1970.

when she found out about her daughter's new career choice:

> I remembered her saying something about how disappointed my father would be . . . If I said I was going to be a physicist, or president of a bank, it would have been different. But I said I was going to be an English major. She could see nothing in that as a future.[5]

Tan's decision to study English and linguistics was another blow to the already strained relationship between Amy Tan and her mother. They did not speak to each other for the next six months.

4

"Squeezing Your Brains Out for Someone Else"

San Jose City College was a two-year college, and after two semesters there, Tan transferred to San Jose State University. She received a B.A. (bachelor of arts) degree in English and linguistics from San Jose State University in 1973. She went on to earn an M.A. (master of arts) degree in linguistics from that same university in 1974. That year she also married Lou DeMattei, who was studying law. He later became a tax attorney.

Daisy Tan accepted her daughter's marriage even though her son-in-law was not Chinese. She had already realized that her daughter might marry someone who was not of their heritage; they had never lived in neighborhoods where there were other Chinese families. Amy Tan had not had many opportunities to meet young Chinese men.

Amy Tan and her husband, Louis DeMattei, were married in 1974.

Tan began studying for a doctorate degree in linguistics at the University of California-Berkeley. The doctorate of philosophy (Ph.D.) is the highest honor a student can earn. Daisy Tan might get to see the word "doctor" in front of her daughter's name after all.

However, Amy Tan left school in 1976 before earning her Ph.D. She realized that "I'd have to do something with my life, not just be a student."[1] She got a job with the Alameda County Association for Retarded Citizens, working as a language consultant for disabled children.

In 1978, Daisy Tan made plans to visit China. By that time, tensions between the United States and China had eased. The move toward a better relationship between the two countries had begun in 1969, when President Richard M. Nixon lifted some travel and trade restrictions that had been in force since 1950. In 1972, President Nixon visited China. He talked with Chinese leaders about areas of agreement and disagreement between the two countries. They wrote down the things they discussed in a paper called the "Shanghai Communiqué."

As communication between the two countries opened up, Daisy Tan saw an opportunity to be reunited with her daughters. It would be her first trip back to China in almost thirty years.

Amy Tan was concerned about her mother's plans. She was afraid Daisy Tan would not come back. She thought her mother might decide, "I've been living with this terrible American daughter, and I've got these three great daughters in China. I'll just stay with them!"[2]

Daisy Tan spent several months in China, but she did return. "When she came back I was so relieved that she still loved me, that she was happy that I was her daughter," Tan said.[3]

In the meantime, Tan's career as a language consultant was moving forward. She accepted a position as a project director with the state education department in California. "I was at that time one of the few Asians in the field, the only minority project director in the country for the Bureau of Handicapped Children," Tan said.[4]

As project director, she served on various boards and attended hearings. Tan soon discovered that she did not like administrative work. It bothered her that one Asian-American person was expected to represent Asian Americans, Native Americans, African Americans, and Hispanic Americans. These groups were very different from each other, and there were differences within each of these cultures. For instance, Tan knew that Chinese immigrants did not have the same needs as the Asian immigrants who were then arriving from Thailand, Cambodia, and Vietnam.

Tan resigned from her job and began working for a company that published an educational newsletter for doctors, called "Emergency Room Reports." She started out as a reporter, then became a managing editor and then associate publisher.

In 1982, one of Tan's half-sisters got a visa to immigrate to the United States. She and her husband settled in a small town in Wisconsin. In China, Tan's sister had been a nurse, and her husband was a surgeon. In the United States, they took what work they could find. Tan's half-sister became the manager of a Chinese take-out restaurant, where she worked six days a week. Her husband got a job in the kitchen of that same restaurant.

It was hard for Tan to understand why her sister had left her homeland, her family and friends, and a prestigious job to come to the United States. It would be several years before Tan fully understood her sister's decision.

Tan left her position at "Emergency Room Reports" in 1983 and began her own business as a freelance technical writer. "I started writing nonfiction as a freelancer the week after I was told by my former boss that writing was my worst skill and I should hone my talents toward account management," she later wrote.[5]

As a freelance writer, Tan wrote sales manuals and business proposals for companies like AT&T, IBM, and Bank of America. She wanted her clients to understand that she was American, not Chinese, so she did not use her own name for her writing. Instead, she chose to write under "non-Chinese-sounding" pseudonyms like "May Brown."[6]

Tan never had to advertise to get clients. Her business grew through word of mouth. It was hard for Tan to turn down clients, and before long, she was working about eighty hours a week.

Daisy Tan understood her daughter's success when Tan and her husband were able to buy her mother a house. "That's really what success is about in Chinese families," Tan says, "it's not success for yourself, it's success so you can take care of your family."[7]

Tan's friends called her a "workaholic," but Tan did not agree. She thought workaholics put in long hours because they enjoyed what they were doing. She was not enjoying her work, yet she still continued. "I kept searching for this thing, this click that would make me feel I had finally done enough—either the right project or working hard enough or earning enough money or feeling that I had written the best thing," Tan explained.[8]

Then came two months when she worked an average of ninety hours a week. "You are squeezing your brains out for someone else, killing yourself," her mother told her.[9] Tan knew she needed to make some changes in her life.

At first she went to a psychiatrist for help. She stopped seeing him after about six months because he fell asleep during their sessions on three different occasions. The first time it happened, Tan was too shocked to react. Then she decided that it must be part of her therapy. "I thought he was trying to tell me I was too passive," she said.[10] Then it happened again. By that time, Tan had noticed that her doctor only fell asleep when she was telling him about something good that had happened to her. "But if I recalled something from my childhood that was traumatic, and I was crying, he was very attentive," Tan said.[11] She decided that he was reinforcing her negative feelings. She gave up psychotherapy and began to help herself.

First she limited her working time to fifty hours a week. Then she started taking jazz piano lessons and writing fiction. Her first writing goal was to complete a short story.

5

"Rules of the Game"

Amy Tan's experience as a business writer gave her a good foundation in the basics of writing. It taught her about meeting deadlines and writing clearly. When she switched to writing fiction, however, there were new things to learn. She began what turned out to be a two-year apprenticeship in writing fiction. During that time she continued to write for her business clients.

Tan started her apprenticeship by reading a lot of fiction, including books by such authors as Eudora Welty, Flannery O'Connor, and Amy Hempel. Although Tan's reading included some male authors, she preferred women writers because she identified more with them.

Tan studied their writing styles, all the time searching for her own voice. Voice is the way a writer tells a story; it is each writer's personal style. Every writer has his or her own voice, but they often find it after studying the styles of other writers. It was Louise Erdrich, a Native American author, who influenced Tan the most.

Tan read Erdrich's book *Love Medicine* in August 1985. The book was a group of interrelated short stories told by different generations of a Native American family. Tan says she was amazed by Erdrich's voice. "It was different and yet it seemed I could identify with the powerful images, the beautiful language and such moving stories."[1]

The idea for Tan's first short story came from an article she read in *Life* magazine. It was about two Chinese Americans who mastered the game of chess at an early age. The young people were called prodigies.

The story Tan wrote did not turn out the way she planned. "As I began to write, the story kept veering from my original intentions—a cerebral piece about chess—to one that concerned the relationship between a girl and her greatest ally and adversary, her mother."[2] What she ended up with was a shapeless, thirteen-page story covering thirty years of a woman's life. She called it "Endgame." The title was a chess term. There are different stages in a chess game—opening moves, the middle game, and the final stage, called the endgame.

Tan sent the story to the prestigious Squaw Valley fiction writers' workshop in California. The story was

Before Amy Tan began writing fiction, she read many books by other authors. She studied their writing styles searching for her own voice, or way of writing.

good enough to get her into the workshop, but it was not ready for publication. "My manuscript was trashed," Tan joked, remembering that workshop.[3] On a more serious note, she said, the workshop was a good experience for her. The best thing that came out of it was that she met Molly Giles there.

Giles had just won the Flannery O'Connor Award for Short Fiction for 1985. That award was established in 1981 at the University of Georgia as a way to give recognition to writers of short fiction.

At the Squaw Valley fiction writers' workshop, Giles read Tan's manuscript. "You don't have a story here," she said, "you have a dozen stories."[4] She went through the manuscript circling all the parts that could be developed into other stories.

Tan had many questions when she went to the workshop. One of them was "Should I continue to write fiction?"[5] At the workshop, she found her answer. "I realized that, yes, this is what I want to do," she said.[6] After Molly Giles had pointed out all the story possibilities in "Endgame," Tan also knew that she had enough material for a lifetime of writing.

Tan went home and rewrote the story. Then she sent Giles the revised manuscript. Giles submitted the story to a small local literary magazine called *FM Five* (later changed to *The Short Story Review*), in which it was first published.

"Endgame" is about a young Chinese-American girl

named Waverly Jong. She is the youngest of three children in her family, and the only daughter. Waverly attends a church Christmas party with her family. At the party, the children receive gifts that have been donated by members of another church. Waverly's gift is a twelve-pack of Life Savers. Her brother Winston gets a model kit for a World War II submarine. Her other brother, Vincent, takes home the chess set.

Waverly's mother is angry about Vincent's present because it obviously is used; in fact, two pieces are missing. When they get home from the party, she tells Vincent to throw away the terrible gift, but he and Winston already are setting up the chess pieces, getting ready to play a game.

Waverly watches her brothers play. To her, "The chessboard seemed to hold elaborate secrets waiting to be untangled."[7] She uses her Life Savers to convince her brothers to let her play too. Life Savers are substituted for the missing chess pieces, and the winner gets to eat the candy.

Waverly is determined to learn to play the game well. She goes to the library and checks out books on chess. At home she studies them, learning new game strategies. She reads about attacking, and about how to get out of traps. She learns that she must "see the endgame before the game begins."[8]

After a while, Waverly's brothers lose interest in chess and find other things to do. Waverly then begins playing chess in the park with an old Chinese man who teaches her even more about the game. He gives names to the moves she needs to beat an opponent—"The Double Attack from the East and West Shores. Throwing Stones on the Drowning Man. The Sudden Meeting of the Clan. The Surprise from the Sleeping Guard."[9] He also teaches her about chess etiquette—"Never hurl pieces into the sandbox after you have lost a game, because then you must find them again, by yourself, after apologizing to all around you."[10]

A man who sees Waverly playing in the park encourages her mother to sign her up to play in tournaments. Soon chess becomes the center of Waverly's life. She enters tournaments and wins many trophies. She goes to sleep at night thinking of new strategies. Her mother no longer asks her to help with chores around the house; she wants her daughter to have that time to concentrate on chess.

Waverly enjoys the attention she gets from playing chess, but she resents her mother's advice on how to play the game. She also accuses her mother of showing off because she is the parent of a chess prodigy. By the end of the story, Waverly sees her mother as her adversary—her opponent in a chess match.

In 1986, Tan was summoned to the hospital. Her mother had been taken there after suffering what appeared to be a heart attack. Tan had already lost her father and brother. She did not want to lose her mother, too. "You always think your parents are immortal," Tan said, remembering that day.[11]

Daisy Tan knew her condition might be serious. She thought about her daughter, who did not know much about her or her life in China. "I might die soon," she said to her daughter. "And if I die, what will you remember?"[12]

Amy Tan made a vow that day: "I decided that if my mother was okay, I'd get to know her. I'd take her to China, and I'd write a book," she said.[13]

The story ended happily. It turned out that Daisy Tan had not had a heart attack. Her chest pain was from an angina attack. (Angina is caused by a lack of oxygen to the heart muscle.) She recovered completely.

In Tan's second short story, called "Waiting Between the Trees," a Chinese woman laments the fact that her daughter knows so little about her. The mother in that story describes her first marriage, a union her daughter knew nothing about. It was an arranged marriage to a man who left his wife in shame while he sought the company of other women.

Tan was encouraged by the publication of her first story. She boldly sent her second one to *The New Yorker*, a magazine known for publishing good fiction. It was rejected.

In the meantime, an editor at *Seventeen* had seen Tan's first story, "Endgame," in *FM Five* and asked to reprint it. The story appeared in the November 1986 issue under the title "Rules of the Game."

In 1987, Molly Giles started a private study group in San Francisco. This was good news for Tan, who had once told Giles to let her know if she ever decided to get a group together in that area. They began meeting once a week, often in Tan's home. The members read their stories out loud, and then the group critiqued them.

Tan says that the purpose of the group was to help members improve their writing. She was not interested in being part of a group that simply praised what she had written. She wanted to learn how to make her writing better. She once expressed her displeasure with another writers' group she had joined. She left that group after one of the writers said, "Well, I believe we're all good writers, and that we should not criticize each other, we should just support and encourage one another."[14]

Tan said that being part of a writers' group helped her keep her writing on schedule and taught her how to edit her own work. It also helped her stay committed to her work. She said that reading a story in front of a group at the risk of being embarrassed meant that she really needed to believe in what she wrote.

Tan's big break came when a literary agent from Del Mar, California, saw "Rules of the Game" in *Seventeen*. The agent, Sandra Dijkstra, said she was interested in representing Tan.

Tan was convinced that she needed an agent when a

friend of hers called to congratulate Tan for having "Rules of the Game" published in an Italian magazine. The story had been translated and printed without Tan's permission or knowledge. Tan thought an agent might prevent something like that from happening again.

Dijkstra wanted to see what else Tan had written, so Tan sent her a copy of her second story, "Waiting Between the Trees." She also sent a note explaining that she was thinking about expanding the story into a novel or making it part of a collection of short stories.

When Tan sent Dijkstra a third story, the agent said, "I think we're ready to sell a book."[15] She asked Tan to put together a formal proposal for a book of interrelated short stories. The proposal was to include a summary of each of the stories.

Tan worked on the proposal, although at the time she did not believe the book would be published.[16] The summaries were short. For one story titled "A Pair of Tickets," Tan wrote, "A woman goes to China to meet her sisters with expectations and discovers something else."[17] Tan said it was all she knew about that story at the time. The common thread in all the stories was that each of the "characters would discover something about themselves."[18]

Tan sent the book proposal to her agent in July 1987. At that time, the title of her book was *Wind and Water*. One of the stories was called "The Joy Luck

Club." Dijkstra liked that title better and suggested that Tan use it for the book.

That October, Amy Tan, her mother, and Tan's husband, Lou DeMattei, left for China, where Tan finally met her two half-sisters who were still living in China. "There was an instant bond," she said. "The way they smiled, the way they held their hands, all those things connected me. I had family in China. I belonged."[19]

Tan also saw how difficult life was for the people of China. She later wrote about her visit in an essay titled "Watching China" that was published in *Glamour* magazine. In that essay, she wrote about attending her niece's wedding in Shanghai. After the wedding, the newlyweds went home to the apartment they shared with the bride's family. Tan told the couple that now that they were married they could get a place of their own. "The waiting list for government-assigned housing is sixteen years," her niece's husband explained to Tan. "We will both be forty-eight years old when we are assigned our own place."[20]

Tan also wrote about the husband of one of her half-sisters who could not attend a family dinner because he was working thousands of miles away. He had been separated from his family for ten years. Tan said he should ask for a transfer. She was told that was not possible. In China, jobs were assigned by the government.

Tan and her mother read a letter from relatives in China. In 1987,
Amy Tan visited China for the first time.

While Tan was in China, her agent was busy trying to find a publisher for Tan's book. Her search was difficult, because she was asking for a large advance. (An advance is money paid to the author before the manuscript is written. Authors can use the money to help with living expenses while they are writing the book.)

Sandra Dijkstra wanted to get an advance big enough so that Tan could give up her business writing and concentrate on the book. The problem was that large advances usually go to writers who are already established. If they have written other books that have sold well, publishers assume that their new book will do well, too. Publishers rarely give a first-time writer a large advance.

Even so, when Tan came back from China, her agent was able to tell her that there was interest in the book. For the next few weeks, Dijkstra negotiated with publishers. By the end of December, she had reached an agreement with a major publisher. They had settled on a $50,000 advance. On December 28, 1987, at age thirty-five, Tan signed a contract for her first book.

6

This Is What I Remember

When Amy Tan learned that her book had been sold, her first reaction was shock. "I was completely stunned," she said.[1]

Her second reaction was much different. She became depressed.[2] Most of the book still needed to be written. She would have to give it her full attention for the next few months. "It was such a wonderful thing, yet it seemed my life was no longer under my control," Tan later told a reporter.[3]

She took about a month to shut down her freelance writing business. She spent the next four months writing the book. "I wrote it very quickly because I was afraid this chance would just slip out of my hands," she said.[4]

While she was working on the book, Tan followed a strict routine. She worked five days a week from 9:00 A.M.

to 6:00 P.M. and took the weekends off. She began each writing session by setting a mood. First she would light incense and then she used headphones to listen to what her husband called "gooey music."[5] "I guess you'd call it New Age music," Tan explained. "It's not as bad as supermarket music, but it is sort of like that."[6]

Once the mood was set, Tan tried to imagine herself in another world. In that world, people came to her and told her their stories. "It was like people telling me the stories and I would write them down as fast as I could," she said.[7]

The stories did not come to Tan in a finished form. Her first attempts were filled with what she called "clever phrases."[8] Instead of writing in a normal, conversational way, she used difficult words that almost no one would understand. She said it was as though she was trying to prove she had mastered the English language. To overcome that problem, she decided to imagine that she was writing to someone in particular. She chose her mother.

Tan had described her mother as a "natural storyteller."[9] "Ask her about the type of mushrooms she had in China, and she'll move into a wonderful story that lasts three hours," Tan explained.[10] Her mother does not just describe events; she also captures the emotions behind the events. Tan wanted to write the way her mother spoke.

Imagining that she was writing the story for her

mother helped the words come easier, but Tan says she still did a lot of revising. Tan estimates she rewrote each page twelve to twenty times.

Tan began revising by reading out loud everything she had written. She wanted the stories to have a certain rhythm. Hearing what she had written helped her establish that rhythm. Sometimes she read directly from the computer screen, but more often she printed out a hard copy on paper to work from. "I'm not an ecologically sound writer," she said. "I figured out that I went through 7,000 sheets of paper writing *The Joy Luck Club*."[11]

Tan did not write the stories in the order in which they appear in the book. Instead, she wrote them as they came to her. "I'd write a mother's story, and then I'd hear the daughter saying, 'Well, let me tell my side of it.'"[12] The exception was the final chapter, which was the last one she wrote.

In the book, Tan tells the stories of four Chinese immigrant mothers and their American-born daughters. When the book begins, the daughters are in their thirties, but their stories go back to their childhoods.

The mothers, or "aunties" as the daughters call them, are all members of the Joy Luck Club. Each week they get together to play mah jong, eat Chinese delicacies, and share stories about their families.

Mah jong is a game which originated in China. It is played with 144 tiles, which are pieces similar to dominoes. The object of the game is to build a winning combination of tiles.

The title story tells about the original Joy Luck Club which was started in China by one of the mothers, Suyuan Woo. The club was begun as a way to survive in that war-torn country. Woo gathered a group of four women, including herself—"one for each corner of my mah jong table."[13] Each of the women had suffered personal losses and faced uncertain futures because of the war. Woo said the women had a choice to make. They could either accept their own deaths with somber faces or they could try to find some happiness.

"So we decided to hold parties and pretend each week had become the new year," she said. "Each week we could forget the past wrongs done to us. We weren't allowed to think a bad thought. We feasted, we laughed, we played games, lost and won, we told the best stories."[14] At those gatherings, before they began to play mah jong, they filled a bowl with money, which each hoped to win. "And each week, we could hope to be lucky," Woo explained. "That hope was our only joy. And that's how we came to call our little parties Joy Luck."[15]

Suyuan Woo later immigrated to the United States. In 1949, she started the San Francisco version of the club. It grew to include husbands. The members soon realized that the same people won each week. It was not luck that determined the winner, but skill. They decided that instead of having members take home their winnings each week, they would pool their money and invest it in the stock market. They believed that making money in stocks was a matter of luck, not skill, and if they all invested together, they would win or lose equally. In that way the Joy Luck Club became an investment club, too.

At the beginning of the book, Suyuan Woo has died, and her daughter, Jing-Mei (June) Woo, reluctantly takes her mother's place at the table. The "aunties" tell June that she has two half-sisters in China. They also tell her that her mother has spent years trying to find those two daughters, whom she was forced to leave behind when she escaped from the Japanese. Suyuan Woo had finally succeeded in getting an address that she believed would lead to her daughters, but she died before she could write to her daughters.

After Suyuan Woo's death, the other women in the club wrote to the address on Woo's behalf. They did not reveal that Suyuan Woo was dead. The women have received a reply from Woo's daughters, who are eager to meet their mother. The members of the Joy Luck Club decide that June must go to China to meet her half-sisters in her mother's place.

The story of Suyuan Woo, her American-born daughter, June, and her Chinese daughters is the unifying thread in the book as June prepares for her trip to China. The stories the mothers tell are about arranged marriages, abusive men, and the hardships of living in war-torn China. The daughters' stories are about careers, bad marriages, and conflicts with their Chinese mothers.

The Joy Luck Club is not autobiographical. "It bothers me that people think this is all autobiographical, as if I just pieced together notes I've been taking all my life,"[16] Tan says. On the other hand, she did use real events and stories her mother had told her. One of those stories was about a woman who was fleeing the Japanese in China. The woman traveled on foot carrying several bags filled with her belongings. As she grew tired, she started leaving bags along the side of the road to lighten her load. Tan used that memory to tell Suyuan Woo's story.

In the book, Suyuan Woo flees from the Japanese with her twin babies tucked into slings that hang from her shoulders. Woo also takes all the possessions she can carry, including bags of flour and rice and two leather suitcases packed with their belongings. As she walks, the suitcases begin to dig into her hands, causing blisters. When the blisters break and begin to bleed, Suyuan Woo leaves the suitcases along the side of the road. She continues walking on, growing weaker with each step. Eventually, she has to leave the bags of flour and rice behind. Now all she has left are her babies. Death, either from exhaustion or at the hands of the advancing Japanese troops, seems certain. To save her daughters' lives, she leaves them along the side of the road, hoping someone will find them and take care of them.

Like Suyuan Woo, Tan's mother was forced to leave her children behind in China, but their stories are not the same. Suyuan Woo has two daughters, while Tan's mother had three. Daisy Tan has never publicly discussed the events that forced her to leave her daughters behind when she immigrated to the United States, but Amy Tan says that her mother's situation was entirely different from Suyuan Woo's.

Another story that Tan used in the book was about her great-grandmother. Tan once asked her mother how her great-grandmother had died. Daisy Tan said, "One day your grandmother went into her mother's room (your great-grandmother was very sick) and cut a piece of meat off her own arm and put it in this soup, cooked it with some herbs, but the soup didn't work and she died that day."[17] In a story titled "Scar," there is a scene in which a woman cuts a piece of her own arm to put in the soup she is making for her mother.

Although Tan used actual events and stories from her past in writing *The Joy Luck Club*, there are also parts of the book that are pure fiction. Tan did not grow up in Chinatown, where some of the stories in *The Joy Luck Club* take place, she does not play chess, and she says that her husband is not at all like the insensitive men in her book. Another difference, according to Tan, is that her mother "is far funnier and more interesting than any of the mothers in the book."[18] However, after Tan wrote *The Joy Luck Club*, she and her friends did form their

Amy Tan in San Francisco's Chinatown. Although Tan did not grow up in Chinatown, some of the stories in *The Joy Luck Club* take place there.

own investment club which they called Fool and His Money (from the saying "A fool and his money are soon parted").

The Joy Luck Club has been called a tear-jerker, but the stories are also told with humor. Tan's first story, "Rules of the Game," is included in the book, and another story, "Four Directions," is a continuation of that mother-daughter conflict. In "Four Directions," a friend of the daughter, Waverly Jong, encourages Waverly to stand up to her mother. She tells Waverly she should just tell her mother to shut up. Waverly is shocked: "you can't *ever* tell a Chinese mother to shut up," she says. "You could be charged as an accessory to your own murder."[19]

In "Double Face," one of the mothers, Lindo Jong, gets a job on the assembly line at a fortune cookie factory. Her job is to put the fortunes inside the cookies. Her coworker interprets the fortunes for her. In one case, the fortune says, "Money is the root of all evil. Look around you and dig deep."[20] Her coworker's interpretation is: "Money is a bad influence. You become restless and rob graves."[21]

Jong thinks the fortunes are nonsense; Chinese people do not say things like that. She does find a way to use the fortunes to win her husband, though.

The Joy Luck Club was promoted almost entirely through reviews and personal appearances by Tan. The publisher sent out hundreds of galleys to reviewers across the country. Galleys are typeset copies of a book that have not yet been proofread. The copies sent to the reviewers were bound and had covers designed by Tan's friend Gretchen Schields.

The reviewer response to *The Joy Luck Club* was better than anyone could have predicted. On March 12, 1989, reviews appeared simultaneously in several newspapers across the country. One, in the *Los Angeles Times*, was by Carolyn See, who wrote, "The only negative thing I could ever say about this book is that I'll never again be able to read it for the first time."[22]

Other reviewers were equally positive. In *The Nation*, Valerie Miner wrote, "Tan is a gifted storyteller who reaches across cultures and generations."[23] In *Library Journal*, Ann H. Fisher wrote, "What a wonderful book! The 'joy luck club' is a mah-jong/storytelling support group. . . ."[24]

Other authors known for writing about their own cultures also gave the book good reviews. Comments by Alice Walker, the African-American author of *The Color Purple*, and Louise Erdrich, the Native American author who had been Amy Tan's own inspiration, were used to promote *The Joy Luck Club*.

Walker wrote:

> In this honest, moving, and beautifully courageous story Amy Tan shows us China, Chinese-American women and their families, and the mystery of the mother-daughter bond in ways that we have not experienced before.[25]

On March 12, 1989, reviews of *The Joy Luck Club* appeared simultaneously in newspapers all across the country. Many of the articles also featured this photo of Amy Tan.

Erdrich wrote, "Amy Tan effortlessly mixes tenderness and bitter irony, sorrow and slicing wit. *The Joy Luck Club* is a fabulous concoction."[26]

Tan was also active in the promotion of her book. She put together a videotape showing herself, her mother, and her husband at a real joy luck club meeting. It also contained footage of them in San Francisco's Chinatown.

The videotape was shown at a sales conference. The reaction from sales representatives was enthusiastic. Marketing agents for the publisher believed that Tan could be successful in promoting her book through interviews and television and radio appearances.

That spring, interviews with Tan were featured in the *Los Angeles Times*, the *Washington Post*, and *People* magazine. She was interviewed on National Public Radio and appeared on television shows, including NBC's *Today* show on May 24, 1989.

There was a lot of excitement about Tan's first book, but there was negative criticism as well. In a review for *New York* magazine, Rhoda Koenig wrote: "*The Joy Luck Club* is lively and bright but not terribly deep."[27]

Other reviewers were critical of the way men were portrayed in the book. In an article for *Newsweek*, David Gates called the men "worthless."[28]

Tan admitted that the male characters in her book were weak. She said this was because readers got only a small look at them at times when they did not seem sympathetic. She said that if she had developed the male characters more, readers would have gotten a different view of them.

This was something she had considered while she was writing. At one point it occurred to her that she needed more balance. She thought about adding a strong male character but she decided against it when she realized that it would take away from what she was trying to do in the book, which was to tell the women's stories. "You have to make some choices," Tan explained.[29]

Until the reviews came out, Tan had never thought of her book as a novel; she thought of it as a collection of short stories. However, the reviewers called it a novel, and the publisher also began to refer to it as a novel. Tan was still uncomfortable with that description. She finally reached a compromise with her publisher. On the jacket flap of the hardcover copy of the book, it is called a "first work of fiction."[30]

Tan dedicated *The Joy Luck Club* to her mother. She remembered that day in the hospital when she had vowed to learn more about her mother and to write a book about their relationship. In her dedication, Tan wrote, "You asked me once what I would remember. This, and much more."[31]

Recalling that dedication, a reporter asked Tan about her mother's reaction to the book. Tan replied, "She's busy going to bookstores to see if they have the book. If they don't, she scolds them."[32]

After *The Joy Luck Club* was published, Tan received a letter from her half-sister in Wisconsin. Her sister wrote:

> I was once like you. . . . I wanted to write stories as a young girl. But when I was growing up, they told me I could not do so many things. And now my imagination is rusted and no stories can move out of my brain.[33]

Tan understood then why her sister had immigrated to the United States, leaving behind her family, friends, country, and work. Tan realized that her own life might have been very different if she had been the one born in China. "My sister and I had the same dream," Tan later wrote. "But my brain did not become rusted. I became a writer."[34]

Tan also kept in contact by mail with her other half-sisters, and in 1990, Tan and her mother made a return trip to China. Since then, Tan and her husband, Lou, have helped her youngest half-sister, Li-June, and her family immigrate to the United States.

7

Fear of the Second Book

Writers are sometimes superstitious about second books. They may have reason to feel that way. After a successful first book, readers and critics are often disappointed with the second one. They think it is not as good as the first one, or sometimes, they say the second book is too much like the first one.

Other writers warned Tan about the response to a second book. One writer said:

> The critics are always worse when the first book was really, really big. . . . With the first, they put you on this great big pedestal. But by the time The Second Book comes around, you realize you're not sitting on a pedestal at all. It's one of those collapsible chairs above a tank of water at the county fair.[1]

Another writer predicted that the second book

would be trashed by reviewers, "especially if the first was an unexpected success."[2]

Their comments were bad news for Tan, whose first book was a huge success. *The Joy Luck Club* was the only break-out novel for 1989. A break-out novel is not expected to be a bestseller, but it becomes one anyhow.

Tan's novel was selling by word of mouth. Mothers gave the book to their daughters, and daughters gave the book to their mothers. They marked passages in the novel that said things they wanted to say to one another. It was a way of communicating feelings they had for each other but had not been able to express.

Excerpts from the book were published in *Atlantic* magazine and in *Ladies' Home Journal*. *The Joy Luck Club* was a finalist for the National Book Award for fiction. It was also chosen as a Best Book for Young Adults by the American Library Association. Translations were published in Italy, France, Holland, Japan, Sweden, Israel, the United Kingdom, Germany, Norway, and Spain. Other foreign sales were planned.

Other writers told Tan not to worry about her second book. They were certain it could not be as successful as *The Joy Luck Club*, so she should just write the second book and be done with it. Then she could go on to her third one. There were no superstitions about third books.

Tan did worry, however. Each time she sat down to write, she thought about the critics and her fans. In an essay for *Publishers Weekly*, she wrote about the troubling thoughts that crowded her mind when she was supposed to be working on her second novel:

> And I would imagine hundreds, thousands of people looking over my shoulder, offering helpful suggestions: "Don't make it too commercial." "Don't disappoint the readers you've already won over." "Make sure it doesn't look like a sequel."[3]

She began to feel the strain of trying to please too many people. The stress was affecting her health. She developed a pain in her neck that radiated down her back. The pain made it difficult for her to sit at the computer to write, so she wrapped heating pads around her waist to ease the pain as she worked. Stress also caused her to clench her jaw. At night, while she slept, she would grind her teeth, and she actually cracked two of them.

Worry was not the only thing that made it hard for Tan to write. She also had to deal with the distractions caused by her rising fame.

There were constant demands for her time. Tan was asked to give speeches, appear at fundraisers, teach at writers' workshops, give interviews, and write introductions for books written by other authors. Tan said that at one point she was getting at least "a dozen requests a day."[4] In the first year after *The Joy Luck Club* was published, she spent nine months on the road fulfilling these other obligations. She never had more than three consecutive days at her computer.

Tan looked forward to days at home doing ordinary things like taking a walk with her husband, Lou, or trying to have a conversation with him while he was reading the newspaper. The changes in Tan's life also affected her husband, but Tan says that he was able to take it all in stride, using his sense of humor to keep things in perspective. He sometimes traveled with Tan when she made public appearances and jokingly introduced himself as Mr. Amy Tan.

The few days Tan did spend at home were interrupted by telephone calls and curious fans. Tan and her husband lived in San Francisco in an eighty-year-old duplex, which they co-owned with the couple who occupied the top half. That duplex had been their home for eight years before *The Joy Luck Club* was published. Shortly after her book came out, Tan began to notice that people were coming by and pointing at her house. From her office in the basement, it was almost impossible for her to ignore them.

Tan did not want to complain about the way fame was complicating her life. She told a reporter:

> It's all so wonderful in a way . . . but there's another side that's all so depersonalized. It's as though whoever this person is that wrote this book, that's got this name on the jacket, walked off the page and just started another life, and I have no control.[5]

Amy Tan at one of many public appearances. She was overwhelmed by the demands for her time after her first book was published.

Tan knew it was time to make some changes. She and her husband moved to a third-floor condominium only a few blocks from the duplex where they had lived. "And if people are still pointing at least I'm not aware of it," she said. "They can't see me and I can't see them."[6] She also changed her telephone number.

In spite of worries and distractions, Tan did begin writing her second novel. She wrote the first eighty-eight pages of a book about a young woman who accidentally killed a judge. Then she gave up that book and started one that took place during the San Francisco earthquake of 1906. She wrote fifty-six pages of that one. She put it aside and began another one. In total, she started six different books and discarded all of them.

Tan was determined to write a book completely different from her first one. "I refuse to write 'Son of Joy Luck'!"[7] she told a reporter for the *Los Angeles Times*. None of the stories she began writing seemed right, however.

The idea for what would become Tan's second published novel came from her mother. Readers of *The Joy Luck Club* believed that the book was at least in part autobiographical. They wondered which of the mothers in the book was Amy Tan's own mother.

In a 1989 interview for *People*, Tan said that no one woman in the book was her mother. She explained that the women represented "different aspects of my mother."[8]

Still, readers persisted in trying to figure out which of the characters was actually Daisy Tan. One day Daisy Tan told her daughter that she was tired of explaining to people that she was not the mothers in *The Joy Luck Club*. She said, "Next book, tell my true story."[9]

Tan liked the idea. Writing *The Joy Luck Club* had helped her resolve many of her conflicts with her mother. On the other hand, Tan realized that there were many things she still did not know about Daisy Tan. She remembered something her mother had said one day: Tan had asked her mother what it had been like in China during World War II.

"I wasn't affected," her mother answered.[10]

Later, Daisy Tan mentioned that sometimes, maybe two or three times a week, they had to run for cover from the bombs. "We were always running," she told her daughter. "We were always scared that the bombs would fall on top of our heads."[11]

Tan reminded her mother that she had said she was not affected by the war.

"I wasn't," her mother said. "I wasn't killed."[12]

Her mother's words made Tan think about the differences between the ways her mother and she viewed the same events. Tan wanted to understand more about her mother's perspective on life.

Tan had also wondered how her mother could have stayed married to a terrible, abusive man for twelve years. She wanted to learn more about the subservient role of women in China at that time. "I wanted to understand what it is like to live a life of repression and to understand the fear that one has, and what you have to do to rise above that fear," Tan told a reporter for *The New York Times*.[13]

Tan knew she would be taking a risk by writing about Chinese-American daughters and their Chinese mothers. It was the same topic she had written about in her first book. Critics and readers might say that her second book was too much like the first one, but she knew that she had to write about a subject that interested her. She decided to tell her mother's story.

When Tan began writing what was to become her second published book, she no longer had any second-book fears. She thought about her first novel and the six unfinished novels she had started and discarded. In her mind, she was now writing her eighth book.[14] For the Chinese, eight is a lucky number, and there were no gloomy predictions about an author's eighth book.

That did not mean that writing the book was easy. There were still frustrations and a lot of revisions. But Tan got the inspiration she needed from an unusual source.

8

Stories That Need to Be Told

In an essay published in *Life* magazine, Amy Tan wrote about the photograph that inspired her as she wrote her second novel. Tan believes that the photograph was taken sometime around 1922. It shows a group of Chinese women and girls who appear to be on some type of outing. They are Tan's ancestors, and the photograph was actually taken at a special Buddhist ceremony after the death of Amy Tan's great-grandmother.

Two of the people in the photograph are Daisy Tan as a child (her name was then Tu Ching) and her mother, Jing Mei, who was Amy Tan's grandmother. Also in the photograph are a cousin, Nunn Aiyi, and Amy Tan's great-aunt, Jyou Ma. Daisy Tan told her daughter that each of the women in the photograph "suffered a terrible fate."[1]

Nunn Aiyi's whole face was scarred by smallpox. At a time when marriages were arranged by families, Nunn Aiyi was considered fortunate to receive two proposals. She turned down an offer of marriage to a lawyer and married the other man.

It was a bad marriage, and she later divorced him. However, she could not find a way to support herself and her young daughter. Eventually she was forced to accept the lawyer's second offer. She became his number two concubine, or third wife. In China at that time, it was common for a wealthy man to have more than one wife. The wives, other than the first one, were called concubines.

The first wife was always the most important woman in the household. Nunn Aiyi's position as the third wife was one of shame. Even so, people said Nunn Aiyi should not complain. "Some people said she was lucky the lawyer still wanted her," Daisy Tan explained to her daughter.[2]

Jyou Ma also had a bad marriage. Her husband, Amy Tan's great-uncle, said that his family had given him an ugly wife. To show his resentment, he insulted his wife by complaining about her cooking. He could be extreme in expressing his displeasure. "One time Great-Uncle tipped over a pot of boiling soup, which fell all over his niece's four-year-old neck and nearly killed her," Tan wrote. "My mother was the little niece, and she still has that soup scar on her neck."[3]

In the *Life* essay, Tan also wrote about her grandmother, Jing Mei. Jing Mei was the wife of a scholar who died from influenza. The young widow was raped by a wealthy man who considered himself popular with women. That act dishonored her, and Jing Mei's only choice was to become his concubine.

The man took Jing Mei and Tu Ching to live with him on an island off the coast of Shanghai. Jing Mei also had a son. She left him behind with relatives. At that time in China, only men were allowed to own property. The man's first family may not have minded Jing Mei's bringing her daughter to live with them, because she would grow up, get married, and leave to live with her husband's family. A son, on the other hand, could be in line to inherit property if the head of the household wanted it that way. For that reason, a son might be resented by the man's first family.

Later, Jing Mei had another son. When the man's second wife claimed Jing Mei's son as her own, Jing Mei committed suicide: "she killed herself by swallowing raw opium buried in the New Year's cakes," Tan wrote.[4] Jing Mei's daughter was only nine years old at the time.

Tan kept that photograph of her family close at hand while she was working on her second novel, *The Kitchen God's Wife*. "This is the picture I see when I write," she explained in her essay for *Life* magazine. "These are the secrets I was supposed to keep. These are the women who never let me forget why stories need to be told."[5]

Daisy Tan thinks her daughter also gets inspiration from another source—Jing Mei. Although Jing Mei died in 1926, Daisy Tan believes that Jing Mei helps Amy Tan with her writing. "She still comes to see Amy all the time," Daisy Tan told a relative, "and tells her these stories."[6] Amy Tan thinks that her mother imagines Jing Mei, dressed as she would have been in 1926, standing behind her granddaughter saying, "Hit the delete button on that sentence, it didn't work!"[7]

Although Amy Tan jokes about that image of her grandmother's direct involvement, Tan says that her grandmother does help her write. "It may sound silly but I do feel there are people, my grandmother and others, who come and tell me things," she said.[8] Tan uses their stories in her writing.

To do research for her second book, Tan read articles about China and World War II in magazines such as *Life* and *National Geographic.* She watched movies set in that time period and studied history books. She also videotaped interviews with her mother.

The first interview with her mother did not turn out the way Tan had hoped. She realized that it was her own fault. She had a tendency to interrupt her mother by saying, "Why didn't you cry? Why didn't you do this? Didn't you think that perhaps you could've left?"[9] She was judging her mother, and each time she did this, her mother would change the story or shorten it.

For the second videotape, Tan just listened. At first, her mother was aware of the camera, but then she forgot about it and let her natural storytelling abilities take over. Daisy Tan spoke dramatically, describing each event in such detail that for Amy Tan it was almost like she was in China with her mother. That experience taught Tan about being a good listener. "It was a lesson on how to listen with your heart, not making judgments and observations," Tan said.[10]

When Tan was about halfway through writing *The Kitchen God's Wife*, a friend called her to say that Tan's second book already had been reviewed. Tan's friend said *The Joy Luck Club* was the topic of discussion at a book club meeting in Columbus, Ohio. At the end of the discussion a woman stood up and said, "Well, I just read Amy Tan's second book, and believe me, it's not *nearly* as good as the first!"[11] Neither Tan nor her friend ever did find out what book the woman actually had read. It could not have been Tan's second book, because she was still writing it.

The Kitchen God's Wife was published in June 1991. In this book, Tan followed the basic outline of her mother's life in China, but she also fictionalized certain events. "I changed many, many things, and added many things," Tan said. "There were things that my mother told me that were too painful to put in—not on my part; they were too painful for her."[12]

The story is about Winnie Louie and her grown daughter, Pearl. Each has a secret that she has not been able to share with the other.

Pearl has not told her mother that she has multiple sclerosis, a disease of the central nervous system. In explaining why she has not told her mother about her illness, Pearl says, "At first I didn't want to hear her theories on my illness, what caused this to happen, how she should have done this or that to prevent it."[13] As time passed it becomes even more difficult to tell her mother the truth. "And now that so much time has gone by, the fact that I still haven't told her makes the illness seem ten times worse," Pearl says.[14] Winnie has not been able to tell her daughter the truth about her life in China before she immigrated to the United States in 1949.

Pearl's aunt Helen intervenes and warns both Winnie and Pearl that if they do not confide in each other, she will tell their secrets. Winnie and Pearl begin to talk.

Most of the book is Winnie's story. She was abandoned by her mother when she was six years old, and she was then raised by relatives. They were kind to her, but Winnie was always aware that she was not as important to them as their own daughter was. They arranged a marriage for her with a man who was abusive. He beat her, raped her, and humiliated her in public. She spent more than a year in prison as a result of her efforts to obtain a divorce. Eventually she escaped to the United States.

All of this takes place against a historical backdrop of world war, a Japanese invasion, and a Communist takeover. In an interview, Tan talked about all the bad things that happened to Winnie: "the most terrible things that happened to that character in the book

Amy Tan at a publishing party following the release of her second novel, *The Kitchen God's Wife*.

happened to my mother," she said. "And I left out things that were even worse than that."[15]

The title of the book came from the fable of the kitchen god. This is the story of a man named Zhang who becomes rich because of his wife's hard work in tending his farm. He does not appreciate her, and brings a pretty young woman named Lady Li to his home. Lady Li eventually chases the man's wife away.

For a while, Zhang and Lady Li live a life of luxury on the money Zhang's wife made by managing the farm well. However, Zhang and Lady Li are too lazy to work the farm themselves, and two years later they run out of money. Lady Li runs off with another man, and Zhang becomes a beggar—roaming the countryside, going from home to home asking for food.

One day he is so weak from hunger that he faints on the road. He wakes up in a kitchen near a warm fireplace. He asks the girl who is working in the kitchen how he got there. She tells him that the woman of the house found him and took pity on him. The girl then says that the woman is walking toward the house as they speak.

Zhang looks out of the window and he sees that the woman is his wife. He hurries to find a place to hide. In his haste, he jumps into the fireplace, and he burns to death before his wife can put out the flames.

When he gets to heaven the Jade Emperor, or ruler, says that since Zhang realized his mistake, the Emperor will make him a god. He becomes the kitchen god—the

76

god who each year decides who is to be lucky and who is to be unlucky.

Tan wondered why a man who had been unfaithful to his wife would be made a god.[16] She says that sometimes "we forget to question why we believe what we believe."[17] According to Tan, the story of the kitchen god is an example of why we need to examine our beliefs.

The last chapter of the book is called "Sorrowfree." Tan chose that title because it showed how Winnie is able to free herself from the sorrows of her past. As she tells Pearl about her life in China, she is able to look at some of the things that have happened to her and to see why she believed certain things. As she examines these events in her past, she is able to understand them and let them go.

Tan says that her mother made that same discovery. For many years, Daisy Tan had kept the sorrow of her life in China to herself, because she was "afraid that people would judge her harshly."[18] She thought people might say that she had deliberately abandoned her children and had contributed to her bad marriage. Telling the stories helped her to get rid of her sorrows.[19]

The gloomy predictions about second books did not hold true in Tan's case. *The Kitchen God's Wife* received rave reviews. Critics thought Winnie was a fascinating character. In a review for *Library Journal,* Ann H. Fisher wrote, "Tan is a gifted natural storyteller. The rhythms of Winnie's story are spellbinding and true."[20] In *Glamour* magazine, Laura Mathews wrote, "The heroine

Amy Tan in her hotel suite at the Carlyle Hotel in New York City.
She was in New York to promote her second novel.

of Amy Tan's second novel is a blunt, penny-pinching Chinatown florist who holds our attention like an Empress in rags."[21]

Many said Tan's second book was even better than her first one. In a review for the *Washington Post Book World*, Wendy Law-Yone wrote, "*The Joy Luck Club*, Amy Tan's first novel, was both a critical success and a phenomenal best-seller. Her new novel, *The Kitchen God's Wife*, is bigger, bolder and, I have to say, better."[22] Pico Iyer of *Time* magazine agreed: "Tan has transcended herself again, triumphing over the ghosts, and the expectations, raised by her magnificent first book."[23]

On the other hand, there were some critics who noted the similarities between Tan's second novel and *The Joy Luck Club*. In a review for *Newsweek*, Laura Shapiro wrote:

> The family she describes is a different one, but once again the tension in the novel is between mothers and daughters, and once again their emotional struggles are framed by a mother's remembered journey through decades of upheaval in 20th-century China.[24]

However, in that same review, Shapiro called Winnie's story an "absorbing narrative" and admitted that Tan "keeps us turning pages."[25]

Although Tan was enjoying success with *The Kitchen God's Wife*, she was once again focused on her first novel, *The Joy Luck Club*. Her next two projects came from that book.

9

The Moon Lady

As a child, Amy Tan liked to look at the illustrations in picture books and to make up her own stories. It seemed only natural that one day she would write her own children's books.

When she started thinking about writing for children, Tan knew she wanted to write a special kind of book—one that could be appreciated on more than one level. It would be a story that younger children would like having read to them, but it also would be a book that older children would enjoy, because they could continue to discover new things about the book.

Her first picture book, *The Moon Lady*, was that kind of story. It was published in the spring of 1992.

The story of the Moon Lady first appeared in *The Joy Luck Club* as an early memory recalled by Ying-ying

St. Clair, one of the mothers in the book. Tan rewrote it as a story for children.

Ying-ying is a grandmother in the picture book. On a rainy afternoon, she entertains her three bored granddaughters by telling them a story about when she was a child.

The story she tells them takes place on the day of the autumn moon festival when Ying-ying is seven years old. That morning Ying-ying's amah, or nursemaid, dresses her in an outfit Ying-ying's mother has made especially for the occasion. Ying-ying asks her amah about the celebration that is to take place that evening. Her amah explains that each year there is one day when anyone can ask the Moon Lady to grant a secret wish.

Later in the day, Ying-ying goes with her family to Tai Lake. They have rented a large boat there for their celebration. Ying-ying says the boat looks like a "floating teahouse."[1]

The family naps during the hottest part of the day, but Ying-ying cannot sleep. She roams about the boat, watching as servants prepare the huge evening meal to be served to the family.

She sees two boys catching fish; then she watches a woman cleaning eels. When the woman finishes, Ying-ying discovers that her special outfit is splattered with blood from the eels.

Ying-ying's amah scolds her and removes her soiled clothes. Ying-ying retreats to the back of the boat.

Evening comes and she sits in the dark, dangling her feet in the water. Suddenly Ying-ying is startled by the sound of firecrackers, which are part of the celebration. In that instant, she loses her balance and falls into the water.

Ying-ying is rescued by fishermen, who take her to shore. She is cold and alone. She wonders if she will ever see her family again. Then she makes her secret wish: Her wish is to be found.

In rewriting her story as a children's book, Tan says, she tried to expand the wish theme. "I wanted kids to wonder about wishes: where they come from and who helps us fulfill those wishes throughout our lifetime,"[2] she explained.

A reviewer for *Publishers Weekly* predicted that young readers would be "mesmerized" by Tan's story.[3] In an article for *The New York Times Book Review*, Ellen Schecter wrote, "Ms. Tan makes details from her Chinese-American background totally accessible."[4] Schecter was also enthusiastic about the illustrations done by Tan's friend Gretchen Schields. "You can almost feel the fragrant red floating teahouse rock on oily waves; hear crickets scratch out their songs on a sultry morning; smell the dark, glossy river that sweeps Ying-ying overboard," she wrote.[5]

Gretchen Schields had been an illustrator for more than twenty years, but *The Moon Lady* was her first experience with a picture book. Schields was born in Japan, and, as a child, she traveled widely to many exotic

Amy Tan holds a copy of her first picture book, *The Moon Lady*.

places, including China, Africa, and Australia. Through her travels, she learned about the myths and fables of those cultures, which prepared her for doing the illustrations for Tan's story.

Schields also shared Tan's view that a reader should always be able to discover something new in a picture book. She once described her favorite kind of books as those with "intricate pictures, in which I could get lost finding stories within stories."[6]

The Joy Luck Club was also made into a movie. Tan cowrote the screenplay with Ron Bass. He won an Oscar award for his screenplay for the movie *Rain Man*, which starred Dustin Hoffman and Tom Cruise.

Often screenplay writers try to condense a story like *The Joy Luck Club* by focusing on two or three characters. Tan and Bass decided to keep all the characters intact. As a result, the movie is two and a half hours long. Much of the story is told in the voice of June Woo, the character who has sisters in China.

The movie was directed by Wayne Wang, who was born in Hong Kong and lived in San Francisco. His most successful film until then was a 1982 movie called *Chan Is Missing*. He followed it with several low-budget films, including *Dim Sum*, a family comedy; and *Life Is Cheap . . . But Toilet Paper Is Expensive*, a Hong Kong gangster movie.

Wang saw *The Joy Luck Club* as a chance to promote a better understanding of the Asian community, but Tan

Amy Tan and her friend Gretchen Schields autograph copies of Tan's first picture book, titled *The Moon Lady*. Schields did the illustrations for the book.

did not want to think of the project in those terms. "I told him I didn't want to just serve as a ramrodder to break down barriers," Tan said.[7]

However, the movie did give Asian-American actresses a chance to play the kind of well-rounded roles that were not often available to them. The large cast included the actresses who portrayed the four mothers and the four daughters of the book, as well as younger actresses who played the mothers and daughters as children. Three of the mothers were played by Tsai Chin, France Nuyen, and Lisa Lu, all of whom had once played the title role in a play called *The World of Suzie Wong*. That role of a Chinese prostitute had been one of the few good parts available to Asian-American actresses in the past.

The movie version of *The Joy Luck Club* was released in September of 1993, and film critics had good things to say about it. In a review for *The New York Times*, Janet Maslin wrote:

> Admirers of the best-selling novel will be delighted by the graceful way it has been transferred to the screen. Those unfamiliar with the book will simply appreciate a stirring, many-sided fable, one that is exceptionally well told.[8]

Critics also praised Wang's directing. In a review for *New York* magazine, David Denby wrote, "Wayne Wang has pulled together some impressive visual skills."[9] A contributor to *Vogue* wrote, "the direct, unashamed,

Amy Tan arrives at the premiere for the movie *The Joy Luck Club*.

intimate manner in which Wang presents the women's stories gives it a special grace."[10]

There was also negative criticism of the movie. In a review for *Macleans*, Brian D. Johnson wrote, "All the women are beautiful, successful and affluent, a fact that is simply taken for granted. And all their men are stupid, evil or, at the very least, unfaithful."[11] Reporting for *Glamour*, Charla Krupp wrote, "Unfortunately, the mother-daughter conflicts are resolved with almost sitcom-like simplicity."[12]

However, both critics and fans agreed that *The Joy Luck Club* touched the hearts of moviegoers everywhere. In a review for *Newsweek*, Laura Shapiro cautioned, "Bring tissues. Bring a whole box, you'll be passing it down the row to your sniffling, nose-blowing, red-eyed neighbors."[13]

In the meantime, Tan had found another way to relax in addition to playing pool. She and other authors, including horror writer Stephen King and newspaper columnist Dave Barry, formed a band called the Rock Bottom Remainders. The group's name came from a publishing term: Remainders are the books that are left over after sales of a particular title have almost stopped.

The band travels in a tour bus and stages shows to raise money for causes such as literacy, First Amendment rights, and aid to the homeless. Tan sings lead when the group performs "Leader of the Pack" and "These Boots Are Made for Walkin'." "We're not musicians," Tan

Amy Tan singing with her band called the Rock Bottom Remainders.

says.[14] Their performances are meant to be fun for both the audiences and the band.

Tan followed her screenwriting debut with another children's picture book, *The Chinese Siamese Cat*. Gretchen Schields again did the illustrations.

In this story, a mother cat tells her five kittens about their ancestors: "you are not Siamese cats but Chinese cats," she says.[15] Then she begins a tale about how these Chinese cats came to have the black markings of Siamese cats.

The mother cat says it is all because of a famous cat named Sagwa, who lived in China "a thousand cat lives ago."[16] *Sagwa* means "melon head," which the mother cat explains is really "another way of saying 'silly.'"[17] It is an appropriate name, because Sagwa always seems to be getting into mischief.

"Sagwa was one of three pearl white kittens who lived in a place everyone called the House of the Foolish Magistrate," the mother cat tells her kittens.[18] The magistrate is in charge of the laws in that area. He is called a foolish magistrate, because instead of passing laws that make the people and animals of his kingdom happy, he makes up rules that force them to bow down to him. He becomes a rich magistrate, because he has so many rules that the people cannot keep track of them all. As a result, they end up paying fines for breaking the rules.

One day the foolish magistrate makes up a rule:

"people must *not* sing until the sun goes down."[19] When the new law is written down, the magistrate leaves the paper out on the table so that the ink can dry. After everyone has left the room, Sagwa jumps down from a shelf, where she had been hiding, and lands in the magistrate's ink pot.

Ink splashes all over Sagwa's face and ears, turning them a brown-black color. Her paws are also covered with ink. She steps out of the ink pot onto the proclamation that is drying on the magistrate's desk. Her ink-covered paws blot out the word "not." The new law then reads, "People must sing until the sun goes down."[20] The magistrate is outraged with this new law, until he realizes that the people are so happy with the proclamation that they are singing his praises. The magistrate then declares that "from now on, all Chinese cats shall have dark faces, ears, paws, and tails—in honor of the greatest of felines, Sagwa of China."[21]

Tan's own seventeen-year-old Siamese cat, Sagwa, was the inspiration for her story. When the cat, which Tan describes as the "meanest cat in the world,"[22] became quiet and did not bite or complain as usual, Tan decided that Sagwa had to be sick and took her to the veterinarian. The doctor said that Sagwa had feline renal failure and might die.

One night, when Tan went to sleep, her concerns about Sagwa's condition were on her mind. That night, Tan dreamed about her cat, and the next morning she

Amy Tan and Gretchen Schields again teamed up as author and illustrator for a second picture book titled *The Chinese Siamese Cat.*

wrote down her dream in the form of a children's story. Fortunately, the real Sagwa survived.

Tan's nieces served as early critics for her book. Her brother, John, a computer technician, has two daughters who were three and six years old when *The Chinese Siamese Cat* was published.

Although Tan loves children, she has made a decision not to have any of her own. "I don't think my life is conducive to having children," she says.[23] She also remembers the pain of losing her father and brother and says that if she had children she would worry about losing them, too. "My mother has said that while losing my father—and they had a very passionate love between them—was hard, there is nothing harder than losing a child," Tan said in an interview. "I would be in fear, constant fear, if I had a child."[24]

Tan's brother and his family live in Calgary, in Alberta, Canada, but Tan has a close relationship with her nieces. She enjoys having them visit overnight so that they can all giggle, gossip, watch movies, and eat popcorn.

The Chinese Siamese Cat was published in September of 1994. That same month, it was announced that Hollywood Pictures—a Disney-owned company—was going to make a movie based on Tan's second novel, *The Kitchen God's Wife*.

10

"Bright Lights, Big City"

The agreement to make *The Kitchen God's Wife* into a movie came after almost a year of negotiations between Tan's representatives and Hollywood Pictures. Specific details of that agreement were not made public. However, according to an article in *Publishers Weekly*, the amount paid to Tan for the movie rights was "in the upper brackets."[1]

The same trio who brought *The Joy Luck Club* to the screen were scheduled to work on Tan's second movie. Tan and Ron Bass would team up to write the screenplay. Wayne Wang was signed to direct. Once again, Asian-American actresses would have an opportunity to star in a movie that an accurate representation of their culture.

In the meantime, Tan was also working on her third

novel, *The Year of No Flood*. Interviewers asked Tan about that book and she told them that it was a story about a missionary from Ohio and a young Chinese boy set during the Chinese Boxer Rebellion in 1900.

The Year of No Flood was never published. Tan said she was not able to finish it because she had talked about the story too much in advance. "It was like opening Christmas presents early and then having to go back later and act surprised. You try to rewrap it, but it's not the same," she said.[2]

Tan learned from the experience and was more secretive about the book that did become her third novel, *The Hundred Secret Senses*. She did not talk to the press about that book until it was actually released in October 1995.

The Hundred Secret Senses is a about a Chinese-American woman, Olivia, and her Chinese half-sister, Kwan. The book covers more than thirty years in their lives going back to when Olivia was only five years old and eighteen-year-old Kwan came to San Francisco from China to live with the family. The book alternates between Kwan's stories of the past and Olivia's more modern story of a troubled marriage.

Kwan believes she has "yin eyes," which means that she can see ghosts and communicate with them. She also believes in reincarnation and tells Olivia stories about another life she lived in China in the 1860s. In that life,

Kwan was a one-eyed servant named Nunumu who lived with western missionaries in a village called Changmian.

Olivia is a photographer, and she and her writer husband, Simon, have a small freelance public relations business. However, after seventeen years of marriage they have separated because of what Olivia sees as Simon's obsession with a previous love who was accidentally killed. Then Olivia and Simon get an opportunity to do one last assignment together—a photo story about China. In an attempt to save their marriage, Kwan convinces them to do the story and travels with them to China as their interpreter.

In China, Kwan's stories of her past life and Olivia's problems in her marriage come together in an ending that Tan says her readers will not like unless they believe in spirits and the idea of reincarnation. "I'm anticipating that there will be readers who won't like the ending," Tan said. "If you don't believe you'll wonder, Why did this happen?" [3]

On the other hand, Tan notes that Americans do enjoy ghost stories. She says "yin" people, or ghosts, are not so much a part of Chinese folklore as they are a part of American folklore. "We certainly have our literary tradition of ghost stories and that's, in fact, what intrigued me about writing a ghost story," she said. [4]

As Tan had predicted, negative criticism of her book came from reviewers who could not accept the ending. In an article for *The New York Times Book Review*, Claire

Messud said that the ending of the story required too much of a "leap of faith."[5] On the other hand, in *Library Journal*, Sheila Riley wrote: "Tan tells a mysterious, believable story . . ."[6] Reviewers praised Tan's storytelling abilities just as they had done with her previous novels. In *Newsweek*, Laura Shapiro wrote "With this book, Tan earns back her reputation and then some."[7]

Tan has been given credit for opening doors for other Chinese-American authors. Actually, Jade Snow Wong was the first to write about the Chinese-American experience in a book called *Fifth Chinese Daughter*. That book came out in 1945. More than thirty years later, in 1976, Maxine Hong Kingston's autobiography, *Woman Warrior*, was published. That book was a feminist look at the Chinese-American experience.

However, no other Chinese-American writers made a big commercial impact on the publishing scene until *The Joy Luck Club* came out in 1989. That year, Tan was the only Chinese-American author on the popular fiction lists. When *The Kitchen God's Wife* came out in 1991, four other Chinese-American writers joined Tan on the spring publishing lists.

Three of those writers were new to publishing. Two of the books were first novels—*China Boy* by Gus Lee and *Typical American* by Gish Jen. The third newcomer was David Wong Louie, with his collection of short stories called *Pangs of Love*.

Author Frank Chin also made the publishing lists

that spring with his novel, *Donald Duk*. Chin had been writing since the 1950s. He was best known for his criticism of other Chinese-American writers like Maxine Hong Kingston, whom he accused of "perpetuating stereotypes."[8] He had also written plays.

If Tan has been a trailblazer for other Chinese-American writers, she has not done it on purpose. Tan says her writing is really about exploring "questions that arise in my life—questions that interest me."[9]

In the past, Tan's questions have been related to the Chinese-American experience. It is a topic worthy of a lifetime of writing. On the other hand, her questions may someday take her in a different direction. Tan does not feel limited to writing about Chinese-American life, but she does admit that she is drawn to that type of story. It is something she can write about from her own experience. "There are no stories in me about bright lights, big city,"[10] she said.

Tan has already earned a place in the history of American literature. There will be more from her in the future.

Chronology

1952—Amy Tan born in Oakland, California, on February 19.

1961—Writes an award-winning essay published in the Santa Rosa *Press-Democrat.*

1967—Tan's older brother, Peter, dies from a brain tumor.

1968—Tan's father also dies from a brain tumor.

1969—Graduates from high school at the Institut Monte Rosa Internationale in Montreux, Switzerland.

1973—Receives B.A. degree in English and linguistics from San Jose State University.

1974—Receives M.A. degree in linguistics from San Jose State University; marries Louis DeMattei.

1974-1976—Does postgraduate study at the University of California-Berkeley.

1976-1981—Works as a language consultant to programs for disabled children.

1981-1983—Works for "Emergency Room Reports," a newsletter for doctors.

1983-1987—Works as a freelance technical writer.

1986—"Endgame" published in *FM Five* magazine and *Seventeen* magazine.

1987—Visits China for the first time; meets two half-sisters.

1989—*The Joy Luck Club* is published.

1991—*The Kitchen God's Wife* is published.

1992—First picture book, *The Moon Lady*, is published.

1993—Movie version of *The Joy Luck Club* is released.

1994—Second picture book, *The Chinese Siamese Cat*, is published.

1995—Third novel, *The Hundred Secret Senses*, is published.

Chapter Notes

Chapter 1

1. David Streitfield, "The 'Luck' of Amy Tan," *Washington Post*, October 8, 1989, p. F1.

2. "My Other Life: The Hustler," *Life*, April 1994, p. 108.

3. Streitfield, p. F1.

4. Jonathan Mandell, "Her Mother, Her Muse," *Newsday*, July 15, 1991, p. 47.

5. Elaine Woo, "Striking Cultural Sparks," *Los Angeles Times*, March 12, 1989, part VI, p. 1.

6. Streitfield, p. F8.

7. Anita Merina, "Joy, Luck, and Literature," *NEA Today*, October 1991, p. 9.

8. Julie Lew, "How Stories Written for Mother Became Amy Tan's Best Seller," *The New York Times*, July 4, 1989, p. 23.

9. Ibid.

10. Dorothy Wang, "A Game of Show Not Tell," *Newsweek*, April 17, 1989, p. 69.

11. Lew, p. 23.

12. Rhoda Koenig, "Heirloom China," *New York*, March 20, 1989, p. 82.

13. Streitfield, p. F9.

Chapter 2

1. Judith Graham, ed., *Current Biography Yearbook, 1992* (New York: The H. W. Wilson Company, 1992), p. 559.

2. Tom Dowling, "Even Mom Can Be Proud," *San Francisco Examiner*, April 4, 1989.

3. Mickey Pearlman and Katherine Usher Henderson, *Inter/View: Talks with America's Writing Women* (Lexington, Ky.: The University Press of Kentucky, 1990), p. 16.

4. David Streitfield, "The 'Luck' of Amy Tan," *Washington Post*, October 8, 1989, p. F8.

5. Kim Hubbard and Maria Wilhelm, "*The Joy Luck Club* Has Brought Writer Amy Tan a Bit of Both," *People Weekly*, April 10, 1989, p. 150.

6. Jonathan Mandell, "Her Mother, Her Muse," *Newsday*, July 15, 1991, p. 47.

7. Anita Merina, "Joy, Luck, and Literature," *NEA Today*, October 1991, p. 9.

8. Streitfield, p. F8.

9. Donna Seaman, "The *Booklist* Interview: Amy Tan," *Booklist*, October 1, 1990, p. 257.

10. Paul Mandelbaum, *First Words: Earliest Writing From Favorite Contemporary Authors* (Chapel Hill, N.C.: Algonquin Books of Chapel Hill, 1993), p. 418.

11. Seaman, p. 257.

12. Mandelbaum, p. 418.

13. Joyce Carol Oates, ed., *The Best American Essays 1991* (New York: Ticknor & Fields, 1991), p. 200.

14. Merina, p. 9.

15. Dorothy Wang, "A Game of Show Not Tell," *Newsweek*, April 17, 1989, p. 69.

16. Eleanor Wachtel, *Writers & Company* (New York: Harcourt Brace & Company, 1993), p. 275.

17. Amy Tan, "Fish Cheeks," *Seventeen*, December 1987, p. 99.

18. Ibid.

19. Ibid.

20. Ibid.

Chapter 3

1. Eleanor Wachtel, *Writers & Company* (New York: Harcourt Brace & Company, 1993), p. 284.

2. Kim Hubbard and Maria Wilhelm, "*The Joy Luck Club* Has Brought Writer Amy Tan a Bit of Both," *People Weekly*, April 10, 1989, p. 150.

3. Wachtel, p. 276.

4. Judith Graham, ed., *Current Biography Yearbook, 1992* (New York: The H. W. Wilson Company, 1992), p. 560.

5. David Streitfield, "The 'Luck' of Amy Tan," *Washington Post*, October 8, 1989, p. F8.

Chapter 4

1. Mickey Pearlman and Katherine Usher Henderson, *Inter/View: Talks with America's Writing Women* (Lexington, Ky.: The University Press of Kentucky, 1990), p. 17.

2. Eleanor Wachtel, *Writers & Company* (New York: Harcourt Brace & Company, 1993), p. 278.

3. Ibid.

4. Pearlman and Henderson, p. 17.

5. Joyce Carol Oates, ed., *The Best American Essays 1991* (New York: Ticknor & Fields, 1991), p. 200.

6. Elaine Woo, "Striking Cultural Sparks," *Los Angeles Times*, March 12, 1989, part VI, p. 1.

7. Barbara Somogyi and David Stanton, "Amy Tan," *Poets and Writers Magazine*, September/October 1991, p. 27.

8. Ibid.

9. Jonathan Mandell, "Her Mother, Her Muse," *Newsday*, July 15, 1991, p. 47.

10. Kim Hubbard and Maria Wilhelm, "*The Joy Luck Club* Has Brought Writer Amy Tan a Bit of Both," *People Weekly*, April 10, 1989, p. 150.

11. David Streitfield, "The 'Luck' of Amy Tan," *Washington Post*, October 8, 1989, p. F8.

Chapter 5

1. Gayle Feldman, "*The Joy Luck Club:* Chinese Magic, American Blessings and a Publishing Fairy Tale," *Publishers Weekly*, July 7, 1989, p. 24.

2. Sally Arteseros, ed., *American Voices: Best Short Fiction by Contemporary Authors* (New York: Hyperion, 1992), p. 155.

3. Mickey Pearlman and Katherine Usher Henderson, *Inter/View: Talks with America's Writing Women* (Lexington, Ky.: The University Press of Kentucky, 1990), p. 19.

4. Ibid.

5. Barbara Somogyi and David Stanton, "Amy Tan," *Poets and Writers Magazine*, September/October 1991, p. 31.

6. Ibid.

7. Amy Tan, *The Joy Luck Club* (New York: G. P. Putnam's Sons, 1989), p. 93.

8. Ibid., p. 94.

9. Ibid., p. 95.

10. Ibid., pp. 95–96.

11. Kim Hubbard and Maria Wilhelm, "*The Joy Luck Club* Has Brought Writer Amy Tan a Bit of Both," *People Weekly*, April 10, 1989, p. 149.

12. Ibid., p. 150.

13. Ibid., p. 149.

14. Somogyi and Stanton, p. 31.

15. Pearlman and Henderson, p. 18.

16. Somogyi and Stanton, p. 26.

17. Ibid.

18. Ibid.

19. Hubbard and Wilhelm, p. 150.

20. Amy Tan, "Watching China," *Glamour*, September 1989, p. 303.

Chapter 6

1. Elaine Woo, "Striking Cultural Sparks," *Los Angeles Times*, March 12, 1989, part VI, p. 14.

2. Ibid.

3. Ibid.

4. Ibid.

5. D. C. Denison, "Amy Tan," *Boston Globe*, July 28, 1991.

6. Ibid.

7. Julie Lew, "How Stories Written for Mother Became Amy Tan's Best Seller," *The New York Times*, July 4, 1989, p. 23.

8. Donna Seaman, "The *Booklist* Interview: Amy Tan," *Booklist*, October 1, 1990, p. 256.

9. Anita Merina, "Joy, Luck, and Literature," *NEA Today*, October 1991, p. 9.

10. Ibid.

11. Barbara Somogyi and David Stanton, "Amy Tan," *Poets and Writers Magazine*, September/October 1991, p. 32.

12. Ibid., p. 26.

13. Amy Tan, *The Joy Luck Club* (New York: G. P. Putnam's Sons, 1989), p. 23.

14. Ibid., p. 25.

15. Ibid.

16. Denis Collins, "Truth and Consequences," *San Jose Mercury News*, July 16, 1989.

17. Mickey Pearlman and Katherine Usher Henderson, *Inter/View: Talks with America's Writing Women* (Lexington, Ky.: The University Press of Kentucky, 1990), p. 19.

18. Somogyi and Stanton, p. 29.

19. Tan, p. 173.

20. Ibid., p. 262.

21. Ibid.

22. Carolyn See, "Drowning in America, Starving for China," *Los Angeles Times Book Review*, March 12, 1989, p. 1.

23. Valerie Miner, "The Daughters' Journeys," *Nation*, April 24, 1989, p. 567.

24. Ann H. Fisher, "Book Reviews," *Library Journal*, February 15, 1989, p. 178.

25. Tan, back cover of *The Joy Luck Club*.

26. Ibid.

27. Rhoda Koenig, "Heirloom China," *New York*, March 20, 1989, p. 82.

28. Dorothy Wang, "A Game of Show Not Tell," *Newsweek*, April 17, 1989, p. 68.

29. Somogyi and Stanton, p. 29.

30. Tan, jacket flap of *The Joy Luck Club*.

31. Ibid., p. 7.

32. Wang, p. 69.

33. Amy Tan, "Watching China," *Glamour*, September 1989, p. 303.

34. Ibid.

Chapter 7

1. Amy Tan, "Angst & the Second Novel," *Publishers Weekly*, April 5, 1991, p. 5.

2. Ibid.

3. Ibid.

4. Ibid., p. 6.

6. David Streitfield, "The 'Luck' of Amy Tan," *Washington Post*, October 8, 1989, p. F8.

6. Mervyn Rothstein, "A New Novel by Amy Tan, Who's Still Trying to Adapt to Success," *The New York Times*, June 11, 1991, p. 13C.

7. Elaine Woo, "Striking Cultural Sparks," *Los Angeles Times*, March 12, 1989, part VI, p. 14.

8. Kim Hubbard and Maria Wilhelm, "*The Joy Luck Club* Has Brought Writer Amy Tan a Bit of Both," *People Weekly*, April 10, 1989, p. 149.

9. Jonathan Mandell, "Her Mother, Her Muse," *Newsday*, July 15, 1991, p. 47.

10. Rothstein, p. 13C.

11. Ibid.

12. Ibid.

13. Ibid., p. 14C.

14. Tan, p. 7.

Chapter 8

1. Amy Tan, "Lost Lives of Women," *Life*, April 1991, p. 90.

2. Ibid.

3. Ibid., p. 91.

4. Ibid.

5. Ibid.

6. Eleanor Wachtel, *Writers & Company* (New York: Harcourt Brace & Company, 1993), p. 283.

7. Ibid.

8. Denis Collins, "Truth and Consequences," *San Jose Mercury News*, July 16, 1989.

9. Wachtel, p. 277.

10. Ibid.

11. Amy Tan, "Angst & the Second Novel," *Publishers Weekly*, April 5, 1991, p. 7.

12. Jonathan Mandell, "Her Mother, Her Muse," *Newsday*, July 15, 1991, p. 47.

13. Amy Tan, *The Kitchen God's Wife* (New York: G. P. Putnam's Sons, 1991), p. 30.

14. Ibid.

15. Mandell, p. 47.

16. Wachtel, p. 281.

17. Ibid.

18. Ibid., p. 288.

19. Ibid.

20. Ann H. Fisher, "Book Reviews," *Library Journal*, June 1, 1991, p. 198.

21. Laura Mathews, "More 'Joy Luck,'" *Glamour*, June 1991, p. 106.

22. Wendy Law-Yone, *Washington Post Book World*, June 16, 1991, p. 1.

23. Pico Iyer, "The Second Triumph of Amy Tan," *Time*, June 3, 1991, p. 67.

24. Laura Shapiro, "From China, With Love," *Newsweek*, June 24, 1991, p. 64.

25. Ibid.

Chapter 9

1. Amy Tan, *The Moon Lady* (New York: Macmillan Publishing Company, 1992), p. 15.

2. Stephanie Loer, "Amy Tan Writes From a Child's Point of View," *Boston Globe*, November 10, 1992.

3. *Publishers Weekly*, July 20, 1992, p. 25.

4. Ellen Schecter, "Girl Overboard," *The New York Times Book Review*, November 8, 1992, p. 31.

5. Ibid.

6. Diane Telgen, ed., *Something About the Author*, Volume 75 (Detroit: Gale Research Inc., 1994), p. 170.

7. John F. Baker, "Fresh Voices New Audiences," *Publishers Weekly*, August 9, 1993, p. 33.

8. Janet Maslin, "Intimate Generational Lessons, Available to All," *The New York Times*, September 8, 1993, p. C15.

9. David Denby, "The Good Enough Mother," *New York*, September 20, 1993, p. 64.

10. "Vogue Arts," *Vogue*, October 1993, p. 216.

11. Brian D. Johnson, "Terms of Endearment," *Macleans*, September 27, 1993, p. 70.

12. Charla Krupp, "The Joy Luck Club," *Glamour*, November 1993, p. 188.

13. Laura Shapiro, "The Generation Gap in Chinatown," *Newsweek*, September 27, 1993, p. 70.

14. Mark Morrison, "Joy, Luck—and a Movie Deal," *USA Weekend*, September 10–12, 1993, p. 6.

15. Amy Tan, *The Chinese Siamese Cat* (New York: Macmillan Publishing Company, 1994), p. 3.

16. Ibid.

17. Ibid., p. 7.

18. Ibid., p. 4.

19. Ibid., p. 12.

20. Ibid., p. 16.

21. Ibid., p. 31.

22. Jeannie Wong, "The Joy of Amy Tan," *Sacramento Bee*, October 6, 1994.

23. Ibid.

24. Ibid.

Chapter 10

1. Paul Nathan, "Rights," *Publishers Weekly*, September 5, 1994, p. 20.

2. Jeannie Wong, "The Joy of Amy Tan," *Sacramento Bee*, October 6, 1994.

3. Erica K. Cardozo, "The Spirits Are With Her," *Entertainment Weekly*, October 27, 1995, p. 84.

4. From a personal appearance by Amy Tan at Buchanan Auditorium, Iowa City, Iowa on November 10, 1995.

5. Claire Messud, "Ghost Story," *The New York Times Book Review*, October 29, 1995, p. 11.

6. Sheila Riley, "Book Reviews," *Library Journal*, November 15, 1995, p. 101.

7. Laura Shapiro, "The Hundred Secret Senses," *Newsweek*, November 6, 1995, p. 92.

8. Gayle Feldman, "Spring's Five Fictional Encounters of the Chinese American Kind," *Publishers Weekly*, February 8, 1991, p. 27.

9. Donna Seaman, "The *Booklist* Interview: Amy Tan," *Booklist*, October 1, 1990, p. 257.

10. Dorothy Wang, "A Game of Show Not Tell," *Newsweek*, April 17, 1989, p. 69.

Further Reading

Hubbard, Kim, and Maria Wilhelm. "*The Joy Luck Club* Has Brought Writer Amy Tan a Bit of Both." *People Weekly*, April 10, 1989, 149–150.

Lew, Julie. "How Stories Written for Mother Became Amy Tan's Best Seller." *The New York Times*, July 4, 1989, 23.

Mandelbaum, Paul. *First Words: Earliest Writing from Favorite Contemporary Authors*. Chapel Hill, N.C.: Algonquin Books of Chapel Hill, 1993.

Mandell, Jonathan. "Her Mother, Her Muse." *Newsday*, July 15, 1991, 42.

Pearlman, Mickey and Katherine Usher Henderson. *Inter/View: Talks with America's Writing Women*. Lexington, Ky.: The University Press of Kentucky, 1990.

Rothstein, Mervyn. "A New Novel by Amy Tan, Who's Still Trying to Adapt to Success." *The New York Times*, June 11, 1991, 13C–14C.

Somogyi, Barbara, and David Stanton. "Amy Tan." *Poets and Writers Magazine*, September/October, 1991, 24–32.

Streitfield, David. "The 'Luck' of Amy Tan." *Washington Post*, October 8, 1989, F1++.

Tan, Amy. *The Chinese Siamese Cat.* New York: Macmillan Publishing Company, 1994.

———. *The Hundred Secret Senses.* New York: G.P. Putnam's Sons, 1995.

———. *The Joy Luck Club.* New York: G. P. Putnam's Sons, 1989.

———. *The Kitchen God's Wife.* New York: G. P. Putnam's Sons, 1991.

———. *The Moon Lady.* New York: Macmillan Publishing Company, 1992.

Wachtel, Eleanor. *Writers & Company.* New York: Harcourt Brace & Company, 1993.

Woo, Elaine. "Striking Cultural Sparks." *Los Angeles Times,* March 12, 1989, part VI, 1–14.

Index

112